The meridian sun of liberty; or, the whole rights
of man displayed and most accurately defined,
in a lecture read at the Philosophical Society
in Newcastle, on the 8th of November, 1775,

Thomas Spence

Gale ECCO Print Editions

Relive history with *Eighteenth Century Collections Online*, now available in print for the independent historian and collector. This series includes the most significant English-language and foreign-language works printed in Great Britain during the eighteenth century, and is organized in seven different subject areas including literature and language; medicine, science, and technology; and religion and philosophy. The collection also includes thousands of important works from the Americas.

The eighteenth century has been called "The Age of Enlightenment." It was a period of rapid advance in print culture and publishing, in world exploration, and in the rapid growth of science and technology – all of which had a profound impact on the political and cultural landscape. At the end of the century the American Revolution, French Revolution and Industrial Revolution, perhaps three of the most significant events in modern history, set in motion developments that eventually dominated world political, economic, and social life.

In a groundbreaking effort, Gale initiated a revolution of its own: digitization of epic proportions to preserve these invaluable works in the largest online archive of its kind. Contributions from major world libraries constitute over 175,000 original printed works. Scanned images of the actual pages, rather than transcriptions, recreate the works *as they first appeared.*

Now for the first time, these high-quality digital scans of original works are available via print-on-demand, making them readily accessible to libraries, students, independent scholars, and readers of all ages.

For our initial release we have created seven robust collections to form one the world's most comprehensive catalogs of 18th century works.

Initial Gale ECCO Print Editions collections include:

History and Geography
Rich in titles on English life and social history, this collection spans the world as it was known to eighteenth-century historians and explorers. Titles include a wealth of travel accounts and diaries, histories of nations from throughout the world, and maps and charts of a world that was still being discovered. Students of the War of American Independence will find fascinating accounts from the British side of conflict.

Social Science

Delve into what it was like to live during the eighteenth century by reading the first-hand accounts of everyday people, including city dwellers and farmers, businessmen and bankers, artisans and merchants, artists and their patrons, politicians and their constituents. Original texts make the American, French, and Industrial revolutions vividly contemporary.

Medicine, Science and Technology

Medical theory and practice of the 1700s developed rapidly, as is evidenced by the extensive collection, which includes descriptions of diseases, their conditions, and treatments. Books on science and technology, agriculture, military technology, natural philosophy, even cookbooks, are all contained here.

Literature and Language

Western literary study flows out of eighteenth-century works by Alexander Pope, Daniel Defoe, Henry Fielding, Frances Burney, Denis Diderot, Johann Gottfried Herder, Johann Wolfgang von Goethe, and others. Experience the birth of the modern novel, or compare the development of language using dictionaries and grammar discourses.

Religion and Philosophy

The Age of Enlightenment profoundly enriched religious and philosophical understanding and continues to influence present-day thinking. Works collected here include masterpieces by David Hume, Immanuel Kant, and Jean-Jacques Rousseau, as well as religious sermons and moral debates on the issues of the day, such as the slave trade. The Age of Reason saw conflict between Protestantism and Catholicism transformed into one between faith and logic -- a debate that continues in the twenty-first century.

Law and Reference

This collection reveals the history of English common law and Empire law in a vastly changing world of British expansion. Dominating the legal field is the *Commentaries of the Law of England* by Sir William Blackstone, which first appeared in 1765. Reference works such as almanacs and catalogues continue to educate us by revealing the day-to-day workings of society.

Fine Arts

The eighteenth-century fascination with Greek and Roman antiquity followed the systematic excavation of the ruins at Pompeii and Herculaneum in southern Italy; and after 1750 a neoclassical style dominated all artistic fields. The titles here trace developments in mostly English-language works on painting, sculpture, architecture, music, theater, and other disciplines. Instructional works on musical instruments, catalogs of art objects, comic operas, and more are also included.

The BiblioLife Network

This project was made possible in part by the BiblioLife Network (BLN), a project aimed at addressing some of the huge challenges facing book preservationists around the world. The BLN includes libraries, library networks, archives, subject matter experts, online communities and library service providers. We believe every book ever published should be available as a high-quality print reproduction; printed on-demand anywhere in the world. This insures the ongoing accessibility of the content and helps generate sustainable revenue for the libraries and organizations that work to preserve these important materials.

The following book is in the "public domain" and represents an authentic reproduction of the text as printed by the original publisher. While we have attempted to accurately maintain the integrity of the original work, there are sometimes problems with the original work or the micro-film from which the books were digitized. This can result in minor errors in reproduction. Possible imperfections include missing and blurred pages, poor pictures, markings and other reproduction issues beyond our control. Because this work is culturally important, we have made it available as part of our commitment to protecting, preserving, and promoting the world's literature.

GUIDE TO FOLD-OUTS MAPS and OVERSIZED IMAGES

The book you are reading was digitized from microfilm captured over the past thirty to forty years. Years after the creation of the original microfilm, the book was converted to digital files and made available in an online database.

In an online database, page images do not need to conform to the size restrictions found in a printed book. When converting these images back into a printed bound book, the page sizes are standardized in ways that maintain the detail of the original. For large images, such as fold-out maps, the original page image is split into two or more pages

Guidelines used to determine how to split the page image follows:

• Some images are split vertically; large images require vertical and horizontal splits.
• For horizontal splits, the content is split left to right.
• For vertical splits, the content is split from top to bottom.
• For both vertical and horizontal splits, the image is processed from top left to bottom right.

THE
Meridian Sun of Liberty;
OR, THE
WHOLE RIGHTS of MAN DISPLAYED
and moſt Accurately Defined,

In a LECTURE read at the PHILOSOPHICAL SOCIETY
in Newcaſtle, on the 8th of November, 1775, for
printing of which the Society did the Author the honor
to expel him.

To which is now firſt prefixed, by way of PREFACE, a moſt
important DIALOGUE between the CITIZEN READER,
and the AUTHOR.

Th' invention all admir'd, and each, how he
To be the inventor miſs'd, ſo eaſy it ſeem'd,
Once found, which yet unfound moſt would have thought
Impoſſible   MILTON.

" Let Thelwall * and Burke from its ſplendour retire,
  " A ſplendour too ſtrong for their eyes,
" Let Pedants, and Fools, their Effuſions admire,
  " Inwrapt in their cobwebs like flies
" Shall Frenzy and Sophiſtry hope to prevail,
  " When Reaſon oppoſes her Weight,
" When the welfare of Millions is hung on the ſcale,
  " And the balance yet trembles with Fate?"

By T SPENCE.

LONDON:

Printed for the Author at No. 8. Little Turnſtile, High
Holborn, Patriotic Bookſeller and Publiſher of that beſt
School of Man s Rights, entitled Pigs' Meat; the End of
Oppreſſion, Grand Repoſitory of the Engliſh Language, &c

---

* See " Sober Reflections" or rather, Lamentations over
the impending Fate of " the veſſel of Hereditary Property,"
by John Thelwall.

Price one Penny.

1796.

PREFACE.

Citizen **PRAY** what is all this you make ado about Land-
Reader lords, and Tenants, and Parishes? We don't
understand you.

Author That is surprifing. I thought I had been very
plain. But none are fo blind as hofe who will not fee. But
the reason why I trouble you with my little publications, is,
that I wish to teach you the Rights of M

Reader Rights of Man! What r—Don't we yet know
enough of the Rights of Man?

Author. No.

Reader No! do you fay? After all that Paine, Thelwall and other Philofophers, and the French Republic have
taught us, do we not yet know the Rights of Man?

Author. No.

Reader. Does not the whole Rights of Man cor fift in a
fair, equal, and impartial representation of the People in
Parliament?

Author. No Nobody ought to have right of fuffrage or
representation in a fociety wherein they have no property.
As none are fuffered to meddle in the affairs of a benefit fociety
or corporation, but thofe who are members, by having a property therein, fo none have a right to vote or interfere in the
affairs of the government of a country who have no right to
the foil, becaufe fuch are and ought to be accounted ftrangers.

Reader Do you then account men born in a country as
ftrangers to it and unworthy of fuffrage, that unfortunately
may have no title to landed property?

Author

Author. Most certainly I do. Especially such men as being afraid to look their rights in the face, have disfranchised and alienated themselves, by denying and renouncing all claim to the soil of their birth, and profess to be content with the " Right of property in the fruits of their industry, ingenuity, and good fortune " This is a right of property that a Hottentot, a Chinese, or a native of the Moon may claim among us, as well as you. Wherefore, as you are content with the property of a foreigner, pray do likewise be content with the privileges of a foreigner.

Reader. I tell you, we have a right to universal suffrage, as well as to the fruits of our labour.

Author. And I tell you, that such Lacklanders as you have no right to suffrage at all For you are to all intents and purposes as much foreigners as the Jews For if birth gave a title many of them might claim as much as you, having been born in the country, and perhaps too through as many generations. So it is not birth but property that gives right of suffrage in a society Sure you do not, by your suffrages, want to interfere in the estates and properties of other men ? You own that the landed interest are the legal propretors of their estates, and of course, the legal possessors of the fountains of life; and yet, by your universal suffrage you want to moulfy to your liking, those very estates which you allow to be private property !— You say that no one has a right to set a price on your labour, yet you want to cramp others in the disposal of what you allow to be as much their right You say you would abolish the right of primogeniture , you would tax all estates according to their value , prevent the monopoly of farms , abolish the game-laws, and thus—and thus—at your whim, you would fashion, reduce, melt, and pare down private property, contrary to your own fundamental maxims of right and wrong. Pray be consistent , and let us know, before you begin, where you mean to leave off. If the Rights of Man be definable, as I believe they are, let them be accurately defined, and then let them be sacred This is the only way to procure unanimity of sentiment, and prevent anarchy Is it necessary that our rights like the rainbow, should always recede from us as we advance? Are they to-day to be subject to this decree, and to-morrow to that , as it pleaseth a few of our leading demagogues, who only wish us to know in part, that they may lead us like men upon a secret expedition. Does not this look as if they longed to fish in dark and troubled waters?

Reader.

Reader. Are we then, because we have no land, to do nothing in our own defence against oppression?

Author. If you don't like the country, and the oppression in it, pray leave it. You have no more right to this country than to any other. While you allow the justice of private property in land, you justify every thing the landed interest do, both in their own estates and in the Government, for the country is theirs, and what you call oppression, is only their acting consistently with their interest, and they certainly have a right to govern their own property, and what affects it. So as by your own confession you have neither part nor lot among them, you are of consequence only strangers and sojourners. Wherefore the landed interest act infinitely more consistently in debarring such unprincipled Legislators from interfering among them, than you do in demanding rights which are inexplicable. Noble architects, truly, who would pull down before you know what to build. Who, to serve some temporary purpose, perhaps of plunder, would put all things in a state of requisition, and then suffer matters to end in as much, perhaps more, oppression than they began. This is not establishing the immoveable Temple of Justice, but erecting the wavering standard of Robbery.

Reader. And pray what do you call the Rights of Man?

Author. Read this Lecture, which I have been publishing in various editions for more than twenty years. There you will see the Whole Rights of Man without reserve. There you will see how far men ought to go in recovering their rights, and where, to a hair's-breadth, they ought to stop.

Of kings and courtiers how the fools complain!
Nor blame their own inord'nate love of gain.
None think that while dire landlords they allow,
To kings and knaves they'll still be doom'd to bow.
None think that each by favouring the deceit,
Himself's a foolish party to the cheat.
Few can be landlords; and these very few,
Must, to succeed, their brethren all undo.
Yet each low wretch for lordship fierce does burn,
And longs to act the tyrant in his turn!
Nor kings alone, but hopes before he dies,
To have his rents, and live on tears and sighs!

PIGS' MEAT.

A LECTURE

Read at the Philofophical Society in New-
caftle, on Nov. the 8th, 1775.

MR. PRESIDENT,

IT being my turn to Lecture, I beg to give fome thoughts
on this important queftion, viz. Whether mankind, in
fociety, reap all the advantages from their natural and equal
rights of property in land and liberty, which in that ftate they
poffibly may, and ough to expect? And as I hope you, Mr.
Prefident, and the good company here are fincere friends to
truth, I am under no apprehenfions of giving offence by de-
fending her caufe with freedom.

That property in land and liberty among men, in a ftate of
nature, ought to be equal, few, one would fain hope, would
be foolifh enough to deny. Therefore, taking this to be granted
the country of any people, in a native ftate, is properly their
common, in which each of them has an equal property, with
free liberty to fuftain himfelf and family with the animals,
fruits, and other products thereof. Thus fuch a people reap
jointly the whole advantages of their country, or neighbourhood, without having their right in fo doing, called in ques-
tion by any, not even by the moft felfifh and corrupt. For upon
what muft they live, if not upon the productions of the country in which they refide? Surely to deny them that right is,
in effect, denying them a right to live —Well methinks fome
are now ready to fay, but is it not lawful, reafonable, and juft
for this people to fell, or make a prefent, even of the whole
of their country, or common, to whom they will, to be held
by them and their heirs, even for ever?

To this I anfwer, If their pofterity require no groffer materials to live and move upon than air, it would certainly be very
ill-natured, to difpute their right of parting with what of their
own,

own, their posterity would never have occasion for; but if their posterity cannot live but as grossly as they do the same gross materials must be left them to live upon. For a right to deprive any thing of the means of living, supposes a right to deprive it of life; and this right ancestors are not supposed to have over their posterity.

Hence it is plain, that the land or earth, in any country or neighbourhood, with every thing in or on the same, or pertaining thereto, belongs at all times to the living inhabitants of the said country or neighbourhood in an equal manner. For, as I said before, there is no living but on land and its productions, consequently, what we cannot live without, we have the same property in, as in our lives.

Now, as society ought properly to be nothing but a mutual agreement among the inhabitants of a country, to maintain the natural rights and privileges of one another against all opposers, whether foreign or domestic; should lead one to expect to find those rights and privileges no farther infringed upon, among men pretending to be in that state, than necessity absolutely required. I say again, it should lead one to think so. But I am afraid, whoever does will be mightily mistaken—However as the truth here is of much importance to be known, let it be boldly sought out, in order to which, it may not be improper to trace the present method of holding land among men in society from its original.

If we look back to the origin of the present nations, we shall see that the land, with all its appurtenances, was claimed by a few, and divided among themselves in as assured a manner, as if they had manufactured it and it had been the work of their own hands, and by being unquestioned, or not called to an account for such usurpations and unjust claims, they fell into a habit of thinking, or, which is the same thing to the rest of mankind, of acting as if the earth was made for or by them, and did not scruple to call it their own property, which they might dispose of without regard to any other living creature in the universe. Accordingly they did so, and no man, more than any other creature, could claim a right to so much as a blade of grass or a nut or an acorn, a fish or a fowl, or any natural production whatever, though to save his life, without the permission of the pretended proprietor, and not a foot of land, water, rock, or heath, but was claimed by one or other of those lords, so that all things, men as well as other creatures who lived, were obliged to owe their lives to some or

other's

other's property; confequently they too, like the brutes, were claimed, and certainly as properly as the wood, herbs, &c. that were nourifhed by the foil. And fo we find, that whether they lived, multiplied, worked, or fought it was all for their refpective lords, and they, God blefs them! moft gracioufly accepted of all as their due. For, by granting the means of life, they granted the life itfelf, and of courfe they had a right to all the fervices and advantages that the life or death of the creatures they gave life to could yield.

Thus the title of gods feems fuitably enough applied to fuch great beings nor is it to be wondered at that no fervices could be thought too great by poor dependent needy wretches, to fuch mighty and all fufficient lords, in whom they feemed to live and move and have their being Thus were the firft land-holders ufurpers and tyrant , and all who have fince poffeffed their lands, have done fo by right of inheritance, purchafe, &c. from them, and the prefent proprietors like their predeceffors, are proud to own it, and like them too, they exclude all others from the leaft pretence to their refpective properties And any one of them ftill can, by laws of their own making (for they are the landlords alone who make the laws) oblige every living creature to remove from off his property, (which, to the great diftrefs of mankind, is too oft put in execution) , fo, of confequence, were all the landholders to be of one mind, and determined to take their properties into their own hands, all the reft of mankind might go to heaven if they would, for there would be no place found for them here Thus men may not live in any part of this world, not even where they are born, but as ftrangers, and by the permiffion of the pretender to the property thereof which permiffion is for the moft part paid extravagantly for, and they are ftill advancing the terms of permiffion, though many people are fo ftraitened to pay the prefent demands, that it is believed in a fhort time, if they hold on, there will be few to grant the favour to And thofe Land-makers, as we fhall call them, juftify all this by the practice of other manufacturers, who take all they can get for the products of their hands, and becaufe that every one ought to live by his bufinefs as well as he can and confequently fo ought Land-makers — Now having before fuppofed it both proved and allowed, that mankind have as equal and juft a property in land as they have in liberty, air, or the light and heat of the fun, and having alfo confidered upon what hard conditions they enjoy

those

those common gifts of nature, it is plain they are far from reaping all the advantages from them, which they may and ought to expect

But left it should be said, that a system whereby they may reap more advantages consistent with the nature of society cannot be proposed, I will attempt to shew you the outlines of such a plan.

Let it be supposed then, that the whole people in some country, after much reasoning and deliberation, should conclude, that every man has an equal property in the land in the neighbourhood where he resides. They therefore resolve, that if they live in society together, it shall only be with a view, that every one may reap all the benefits from their natural rights and privileges possible. Therefore, a day is appointed on which the inhabitants of each parish meet, in their respective parishes, to take their long-lost rights into possession, and to form themselves into corporations. So then each parish becomes a corporation, and all the men who are inhabitants become members or burgers. The land with all that appertains to it, is in every parish, made the property of the corporation or parish, with as ample power to let, repair or alter all, or any part thereof, as a lord of the manor enjoys over his lands, houses &c but the power of alienating the least morsel, in any manner from the parish, either at this or any time hereafter, is denied. For it is solemnly agreed to, by the whole nation that a parish that shall either sell, or give away, any part of its landed property shall be looked upon with as much honor and detestation, and used by them as if they had sold all their children to be slaves, or massacred them with their own hands. Thus are there no more nor other land ords, in the whole country than the parishes, and each of them is sovereign landlord of its own territories.

O' hearken! ye besotted sons of men. By this one bold resolve your chains are eternally broken, and your enemies annihilated. By this one resolve the power, the pride, and the arrogance of the landed interest, those universal and never ceasing scourges and plunderers of your race, are instantaneously and for ever broken and cut off. For being thus deprived and shorn of their revenues they becom like shorn Samson, weak as other men; weak as the poor dejected wretches whom they have so long been grinding and treading under foot.

There you may behold the rent, which the people have
paid

paid into the parish treasuries employed by each parish in paying the government so much per pound to make up the sum, what the parliament or national representatives at any time think requisite, in maintaining and relieving its own poor, and people out of work, in paying the necessary Officers their salaries, in building, repairing, and adorning its houses, bridges, and other structures, in making and maintaining convenient and delightful streets, highways, and passages both for foot and carriages, in making and maintaining canals, and other conveniences for trade and navigation, in planting and taking in waste grounds, in providing and keeping up a magazine of ammunition and all sorts of arms sufficient for all its inhabitants in case of danger from enemies, in premiums for the encouragement of agriculture, or any thing else thought worthy of encouragement, and, in a word, in doing whatever the people think proper, and not as formerly, to support and spread luxury, pride, and all manner of vice. As for corruption in elections, it has now no being or effect among them, all affairs to be determined by voting either in a full meeting of a parish, its committees or in the house of Representatives, are done by balloting, so that votings, or elections among them, occasion no animosities, for none need to let another know for which side he votes, all that can be done, therefore, to gain a majority of votes for any thing, is to make it appear in the best light possible by speaking or writing

Among them government does not meddle in every task, but on the contrary, allows to each parish the power of putting the laws in force in all cases, and does not interfere, but when they act manifestly to the prejudice of society, and the rights and liberties of mankind as established in their glorious constitution and laws. For the judgment of a parish may be as much depended upon as that of a house of lords, because they have as little to fear from speaking or voting according to truth, as they

A certain number of neighbouring parishes, chuse delegates to represent them in Parliament, Senate, or Congress and each of them pays equally towards their maintainance. They are chosen thus all the candidates are proposed in every parish on the same day, when the election by balloting immediately proceeds in all the parishes at once, to prevent too great a concourse at one place, and they who are found to have the majority on a proper survey of the several pole books are acknowledged to be their representatives.

A man

A man by dwelling a whole year in any parish becomes a parishioner, or member of its corporation, and retains that privilege, till he lives a full year in some other, when he becomes a member in that parish and immediately loses all his right to the former for ever, unless he chuse to go back and recover it, by dwelling again a full year there. Thus none can be a member of two parishes at once, and yet a man is always a member of one though he move ever so oft.

If in any parish should be dwelling strangers from foreign nations, or people from distant parishes who by sickness or other casualties should become so necessitous as to require relief before they have acquired a settlement by dwelling a full year therein, then this parish, as if it were their proper settlement, immediately takes them under its humane protection, and the expence thus incurred by any parish in providing for those not properly their own poor, being taken an account of, is deducted by the parish, out of the first payment made to the state. Thus poor strangers being the poor of the State, are not looked upon by their new neighbours where they are come to reside with an envious eye lest they should become burthensome, neither are the poor harassed about in the extremity of distress and perhaps in a dying condition, to gratify the litigiousness of parishes.

All the men in the parish, at times of their own chusing, repair together to a field for that purpose, with their officers, arms, banners, and all sorts of martial music, in order to learn or retain the complete art of war, there they become soldiers! Yet not to molest their neighbours unprovoked, but to be able to defend what none have a right to dispute their title to the enjoyment of, and woe be to them who occasion them to do this! they would use them worse than highwaymen, or pirates, if they got them in their power.

There is no army kept in pay among them, in times of peace: as all have a property in their country to defend, they are alike ready to run to arms when their country is in danger; and when an army is to be sent abroad, it is soon raised, of ready trained soldiers, either as volunteers, or by casting lots in each parish for so many men.

Besides, as each man has a vote in all the affairs of his parish, and for his own sake must wish well to the public, the land is let in very small farms, which makes employment for a greater number of hands, and makes more victualling of all kinds be raised.

There

There are no tolls or taxes of any kind paid among them, by native or foreigner, but the aforesaid rent. The government, poor, roads, &c &c. as said before, are all maintained by the parishes with the rent, on which account, all wares, manufactures, allowable trade, employments, or actions, are entirely duty-free. Freedom to do any thing whatever cannot there be bought, a thing is either entirely prohibited as theft or murder, or entirely free to every one without tax or price.

When houses, lands, or any tenements become vacant they are let publicly by the parish officers in seven years leases to the best bidder. This way prevents collusion to the prejudice of the parish revenue and likewise prevents partiality.

Methinks I now behold the parish republics, like fraternal or benefit societies each met at quarter-day to pay their rents and to settle their accounts as well with the state as with all their parochial officers and workmen, their several accounts having been examined some days before.

On that day which is always a day, not, as now of sorrow, but of gladness, when the rents are all paid in, and the sum total proclaimed, the first account to be settled is the demand made by the national representation of so much per pound in behalf of the state, which sum is set apart to be sent to the national treasury. Another sum is also set apart for the parish treasury to answer contingencies till next quarter-day. Next the salaries of the parish officers are paid. Then are paid the respective bills of their workmen as masons, bricklayers, carpenters, glaziers, painters, &c who have been employed in building or repairing the houses and other parish buildings. After these come the paviors, lamplighters watchmen, scavengers, and all the other work people employed by the parish, to receive their demands, until none remain. Then the residue of the public money or rents after all public demands are thus satisfied, which is always two-thirds, more or less, of the whole sum collected, comes lastly to be disposed of, which is the most pleasant part of the business to every one. The number of parishioners, and the sum which is left to be divided among them being announced, each without respect of persons is sent home joyfully with an equal share.

> So if by sickness or mischance,
>   To poverty some want,
> Their dividend of rents will come,
>   To set them up again.

Though

Though I have only spoke of parishioners receiving dividends, which may be understood as if men only were meant to share the residue of the rents, yet I would have no objection, if the people thought proper, to divide it among the whole number of souls, male and female, married and single in a parish from the infant of a day old to the second infantage of hoary hairs. For as all of every age, legitimate and illegitimate, have a right to live on the public common, and as that common, for the sake of cultivation, must be let out for rent, that rent, then, ought to be equally enjoyed by every human being, instead of the soil which they are thus deprived of.

But what makes this prospect yet more glorious is, that after this empire of right and reason is thus established it will stand for ever. Force and corruption attempting its downfall shall equally be baffled, and all other nations struck with wonder and admiration at its happiness and stability, shall follow the example, and thus the whole earth shall at last be happy and live like brethren.

F I N I S

14 JY 6(

An Important QUERY.

Has the universal confusion and agitation of political opinions, occasioned by the French Revolution, produced no publication lately, by containing a brief and clear solution of all the great political problems, to outlive the present ferment, and become a permanent and standing School of Man's Rights to rising Generations?

Answer. Yes, there is one that was compiled and published with that extensive view, and whose solid worth will daily become more apparent, as the temporary and tautological productions of the moment sink into oblivion. This Publication is entitled, in conformity to the phrases of the times, "Pigs' Meat, or Lessons for the Swinish Multitude," consisting of 3 volumes duodecimo, price 2s 6d. each, half bound. Nothing but the title is local and temporary, and it may, perhaps, hereafter be more generally printed and known under the title of the Universal School of Man's Rights.